Pupil Book 1

Comprehension

Skills

Author: Abigail Steel

William Collins' dream of knowledge for all began with the publication of his first book in 1819.

A self-educated mill worker, he not only enriched millions of lives, but also founded a flourishing publishing house. Today, staying true to this spirit, Collins books are packed with inspiration, innovation and practical expertise. They place you at the centre of a world of possibility and give you exactly what you need to explore it.
Collins. Freedom to teach.

Published by Collins
An imprint of HarperCollins*Publishers*
The News Building
1 London Bridge Street
London
SE1 9GF

Browse the complete Collins catalogue at
www.collins.co.uk

© HarperCollins*Publishers* Limited 2017

10 9 8 7 6 5 4

ISBN 978-0-00-823634-2

Publishing Director: Lee Newman
Publishing Manager: Helen Doran
Senior Editor: Hannah Dove
Project Manager: Emily Hooton
Author: Abigail Steel
Development Editor: Hannah Hirst-Dunton
Copy-editor: Catherine Dakin
Proofreader: Tracy Thomas
Cover design and artwork: Amparo Barrera and Ken Vail Graphic Design
Internal design concept: Amparo Barrera
Typesetter: Jouve India Private Ltd
Illustrations: Advocate Art
Production Controller: Rachel Weaver
Printed and bound by Martins the Printers

Acknowledgements

The publishers wish to thank the following for permission to reproduce content. Every effort has been made to trace copyright holders and to obtain their permission for the use of copyright materials. The publishers will gladly receive any information enabling them to rectify any error or omission at the first opportunity.

HarperCollins Publishers Ltd for extracts on page 4 from *One Snowy Night* by Nick Butterworth, copyright © Nick Butterworth, 2011; page 6 from *Hansel and Gretel* by Malachy Doyle, copyright © Malachy Doyle, 2006; and page 8 from *The King of the Forest* by Saviour Pirotta, copyright © Saviour Pirotta, 2012. Reproduced by permission of HarperCollins Publishers Ltd; David Higham Associates Ltd for the poem on page 10 'Cats' by Eleanor Farjeon, published in *Blackbird Has Spoken*, Macmillan, 1999. Reproduced by permission of David Higham Associates Ltd; HarperCollins Publishers Ltd for the poem on page 13 'Honey Bear' by Elizabeth Lang, published in *The Book of a Thousand Poems* edited by J. Murray Macbain, copyright © Elizabeth Lang, 1986. Reproduced by permission of HarperCollins Publishers Ltd; Usborne Publishing Ltd for an extract on page 17 from *First Encyclopedia of the Human Body*. Reproduced by permission of Usborne Publishing, 83–85 Saffron Hill, London EC1N 8RT, UK, www.usborne.com, copyright © 2011 Usborne Publishing Ltd; HarperCollins Publishers Ltd for an extract on page 19 from *A Day Out* by Petr Horáček, copyright © HarperCollins Publishers Ltd 2013; Bonnier Publishing for an extract on page 21 from *Man on the Moon (A Day in the Life of Bob)* by Simon Bartram, p.5, 2002. Reproduced with permission; HarperCollins Publishers Ltd for an extract on page 23 from *Your Nose* by Nick Arnold and Maurizio De Angelis, copyright © Nick Arnold and Maurizio De Angelis, 2013; extract on page 25 from *It Was a Cold Dark Night* by Tim Hopgood, copyright © Tim Hopgood 2010; extract on page 27 from *Hand Play* by Elspeth Graham, copyright © HarperCollins Publishers Ltd 2013; extract on page 29 from *The Fox and the Stork* by Simon Puttock, copyright © Simon Puttock 2013; extract on page 31 from *The Lion and the Mouse* by Anthony Robinson, copyright © Anthony Robinson 2010; extract on page 33 from *Time for School* by Wendy Cope, copyright © Wendy Cope 2013; extract on page 35 from *Zog and Zebra* by Mal Peet and Elspeth Graham, copyright © HarperCollins Publishers Ltd 2013; extract on page 37 from *The Lonely Penguin* by Petr Horáček, copyright © HarperCollins Publishers Ltd 2011; extract on page 39 from *Bart the Shark* by Paul Shipton, copyright © HarperCollins Publishers Ltd 2006; extract on page 41 from *Jack and the Beanstalk* by Caryl Hart, copyright © Caryl Hart 2013; extract on page 43 from *The Prince and the Parsnip* by Vivian French, copyright © Vivian French 2013; extract on page 45 from *The Hare and the Tortoise* by Melanie Williamson, copyright © Melanie Williamson 2013; extract on page 47 from *The Rainforest at Night* by Nic Bishop, copyright © Nic Bishop 2006; and extract on page 49 from *The Sun and the Moon* by Paul Shipton, copyright © Paul Shipton 2006. Reproduced by permission of HarperCollins Publishers Ltd.

The publishers would like to thank the following for permission to reproduce photographs:

p.23 Shanta Giddens/Shutterstock, p.24 leungchopan/Shutterstock, p.49 (t) ESA & NASA, p.49 (b) NASA.

Contents

Key stories: 'One Snowy Night'

From 'One Snowy Night' by Nick Butterworth

It's cold in the park in winter. But Percy the park keeper doesn't mind.

He puts on his warm coat and his big scarf and wears two pairs of woolly socks inside his wellington boots.

Percy likes to be out in the fresh air.

In the middle of the park there is a little hut. This is where Percy lives.

When it gets too cold to be outside, Percy goes into his hut where it's cosy and warm.

Get started

Find the sentences in the story and write the missing words.

1. It's cold in the park in _Winter_.

2. But _Percy_ the park keeper doesn't mind.

3. Percy likes to be out in the _fresh_ air.

4. In the _middle_ of the park there is a little hut.

Try these

Answer these questions. Use the story to help you.

1. What is Percy's job?
2. Where does Percy live?
3. What has Percy got on his feet?
4. What is it like in the hut?

Now try these

1. What do you think the park is like in summer?

2. Draw a picture of Percy in his hut.

3. Draw and label all the things Percy puts on to keep warm. With a partner, add other things he could wear.

Fairy stories: 'Hansel and Gretel'

From 'Hansel and Gretel' by Malachy Doyle

"There is no food," said the woodman.

"How will we eat?"

"Take Hansel and Gretel for a walk in the Brown Wood," said his wife, "and leave them."

"No!" said the woodman. "I cannot!"

"You must, or we will all die!" cried his wife.

So the woodman took Hansel and Gretel into the Brown Wood.

He gave the boy and girl some cake to eat.

But Hansel put it in his pocket and dropped little bits all along the way.

Get started

Find the sentences in the story and write the missing words.

1. "There is no _____," said the woodman.

2. "How will we _____?"

3. So the woodman took Hansel and _____ into the Brown Wood.

4. He gave the boy and girl some _____ to eat.

Try these

Answer these questions. Use the story to help you.

1. Who is in the story?

2. What is the problem?

3. Where did the woodman take the children?

4. What did he give them?

Now try these

1. Why do you think Hansel dropped bits of cake?

2. Draw a picture of Hansel dropping bits of cake.

3. Draw and label Hansel and Gretel when they are left in the wood. With a partner, plan what they can do next. Add a sentence to your picture to explain what their plan is.

Traditional tales: 'The King of the Forest'

From 'The King of the Forest' by Saviour Pirotta

A fox was having a nap. Suddenly a tiger leapt out at him.

"I've got you!"

The fox trembled. How could he save himself?

But then the fox had an idea. He said to the tiger, "How dare you touch the king of the forest?"

The tiger said, "The lion is the king of the forest."

The fox replied, "Everyone bows down before me now. Let go of me, and I'll show you."

Get started

Find the sentences in the tale and write the missing words.

1. A _____ was having a nap.

2. Suddenly a tiger _____ out at him.

3. But then the fox had an _____.

4. "Everyone _____ down before me now."

Try these

Answer these questions. Use the tale to help you.

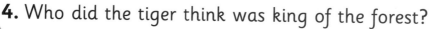

1. What was the fox doing before the tiger leapt out?

2. What did the fox do when the tiger leapt out?

3. Who did the fox say he was?

4. Who did the tiger think was king of the forest?

Now try these

1. Do you think the fox's plan is clever? Why?

2. Draw a picture of the fox having a nap.

3. Draw a picture of the fox and the tiger in the forest. With a partner, think of what they will say next. Add speech bubbles to show what they will say.

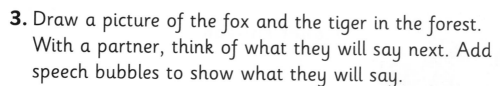

Rhymes and poems: 'Cats'

Cats sleep
Anywhere,
Any table,
Any chair,
Top of piano,
Window-ledge,
In the middle,
On the edge,
Open drawer,
Empty shoe,
Anybody's
Lap will do
Fitted in a cardboard box
In the cupboard
With your frocks –
Anywhere!
They don't care!
Cats sleep
Anywhere.

Eleanor Farjeon

Get started

Find the lines in the poem and write the missing words.

1. Cats sleep _____

2. Any table, Any _____

3. Anybody's _____ will do

4. Fitted in a _____ box

Try these

Answer these questions. Use the poem to help you.

1. What is in the cupboard with the cat?

2. Where on the window-ledge will cats sleep?

3. Where do cats sleep? List three places.

4. What word in the poem sounds like 'ledge'?

Now try these

1. Why do you think cats will sleep anywhere?

2. Draw a picture of a cat sleeping in a shoe.

3. As a class, say the poem aloud. Repeat the poem and try to remember the words when your teacher pauses.

   Then write down the pairs of words that sound the same. Read the pairs of words aloud to a partner. With your partner, add other words that sound like them.

Rhymes and poems: 'Honey Bear'

There was a big bear
Who lived in a cave;
His greatest love
Was honey.
He had two pence a week
Which he never could save,
So he never had
Any money.
I bought him a money box
Red and round,
In which to put
His money.
He saved and saved
Till he got a pound,
Then he spent it all
On honey.

Elizabeth Lang

Get started

Find the lines in the poem and write the missing words.

1. There was a big _____ Who lived in a cave

2. His greatest _____ Was honey

3. I bought him a _____ box

4. He _____ and saved

13

Try these

Answer these questions. Use the poem to help you.

1. What did the bear love most?

2. How much money did the bear get each week?

3. What did the money box look like?

4. What word in the poem sounds like 'round'?

Now try these

1. Why do you think the bear could never save?

2. Draw a picture of the bear eating honey.

3. As a class, say the poem aloud. Repeat the poem and try to remember the words when your teacher pauses.

With a partner, list things that make you want to spend your money. Draw a poster to remind you and the bear to 'Save, Don't Spend!'

Rhymes and poems: 'A Chubby Little Snowman'

A chubby little snowman
Had a carrot nose;
Along came a rabbit
And what do you
suppose?
That hungry little bunny,
Looking for his lunch,
ATE the snowman's carrot
nose ...
Nibble, nibble, CRUNCH!

Anon

Get started

Find the lines in the poem and write the missing words.

1. A chubby little _____

2. Had a _____ nose

3. That _____ little bunny

4. ATE the snowman's carrot
_____

Try these

Answer these questions. Use the poem to help you.

1. Who had a carrot nose?

2. Who was hungry?

3. What did the bunny do to the snowman?

4. What does 'chubby' mean? Ask a teacher for help if you need to.

Now try these

1. How did the bunny feel before he ate the carrot nose? How do you think he felt after he ate it?

2. Draw and label a picture of the snowman before the bunny comes.

3. As a class, say the poem aloud. Repeat the poem and try to remember the words when your teacher pauses.

Draw a picture of the snowman after the bunny has taken his carrot nose. With a partner, think about what happens next. Add a sentence to your picture to explain what happens next.

Reading instructions: 'Test your taste buds'

You will need: grated apple, grated pear and grated carrot in three separate bowls; a spoon; a blindfold.

1. Put on the blindfold and hold your nose.

2. Ask a friend to feed you a spoonful from each of the three bowls. Can you tell which food is which?

3. Try the same thing again without holding your nose. This time, it should be much easier to tell the foods apart.

Get started

Find the sentences in the instructions and write the missing words.

1. Put on the _____ and hold your nose.

2. Ask a friend to feed you a _____ from each of the three bowls.

3. Can you tell which _____ is which?

4. Try the same thing again without _____ your nose.

Try these

Answer these questions. Use the instructions to help you.

1. What do you need for this test?

2. How many instructions are there?

3. What should you do before your friend feeds you?

4. How do you know in what order to do the instructions?

Now try these

1. What sense is stopped when you hold your nose?

2. Draw and label a picture of two friends doing this test.

3. With a partner, do this test. Write a sentence about what you found out.

Story: 'A Day Out'

From 'A Day Out' by Petr Horáček

The bird flies past the farm. But wait ... Look! A fox is lying in the bush. The fox is looking at the bird.

The fox runs after the bird, but it is too slow. He cannot reach the fast bird. The bird flies to the wood. Just in time.

It is a deep, dark wood. But wait ... Look out! A stag is standing by the tree. It is time to fly home.

Get started

Find the sentences in the story and write the missing words.

1. The bird flies _____ the farm.

2. A fox is lying in the _____.

3. He cannot _____ the fast bird.

4. It is a deep, _____ wood.

Try these

Answer these questions. Use the story to help you.

1. Who flew past the farm?

2. Where was the fox?

3. What did the fox do?

4. What did the bird see in the deep, dark wood?

Now try these

1. Why do you think the bird decides it is time to fly home?

2. Draw a picture of the bird flying past the farm.

3. Draw and label a picture of the bird in the wood. With a partner, come up with a sentence to show what the bird is thinking. Add the sentence to your picture.

Reading recounts: 'Man on the Moon'

From 'Man on the Moon' by Simon Bartram

This is where Bob lives. Every morning he rises at six o'clock. He has a cup of tea and two eggs for breakfast, before leaving for the rocket launch-pad. On the way he stops to buy a newspaper and some chocolate toffees.

He's on his way to work …

… on the MOON!

Get started

Find the sentences in the recount and write the missing words.

1. Every _____ he rises at six o'clock.

2. He has a cup of tea and two eggs for _____, before leaving for the rocket launch-pad.

3. On the way he stops to _____ a newspaper and some chocolate toffees.

4. He's on his way to _____ … … on the MOON!

Try these

Answer these questions. Use the recount to help you.

1. What does Bob do first in the morning?

2. What does Bob get to read on the way to work?

3. What sweets does Bob like?

4. Where does Bob work?

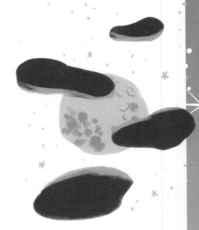

Now try these

1. How do you think Bob feels about his job?

2. Draw a picture of Bob eating breakfast.

3. Draw a picture of yourself eating breakfast. What are you eating? Add a sentence to your picture to explain what you are eating. With a partner, talk about what else you do in the morning. Add one more sentence to your picture to explain what else you do in the morning.

Reading reports: 'Your Nose'

From 'Your Nose' by Nick Arnold and Maurizio De Angelis

A nose can be big. A nose can be small. Your nose is hard on top and soft at the end. It hurts when you bang your nose. Your nose has two nostrils. There are hairs in the nostrils and they are wet inside. You have snot in your nose.

Get started

Find the sentences in the report and write the missing words.

1. A _____ can be big.

2. Your nose is hard on _____ and soft at the end.

3. It _____ when you bang your nose.

4. Your nose has two _____.

Try these

Answer these questions. Use the report to help you.

1. Where on the body is your nose?

2. What size can a nose be?

3. Which part of the nose is soft?

4. What do nostrils have inside?

Now try these

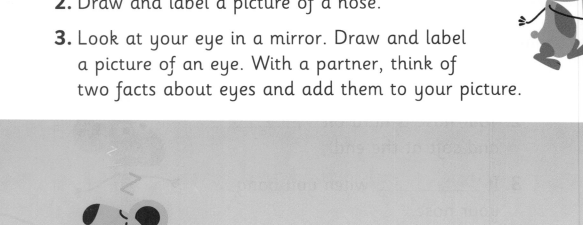

1. Why do you think you have a nose?

2. Draw and label a picture of a nose.

3. Look at your eye in a mirror. Draw and label a picture of an eye. With a partner, think of two facts about eyes and add them to your picture.

Key stories: 'It Was a Cold, Dark Night'

From 'It Was a Cold, Dark Night' by Tim Hopgood

It was a cold, dark night and the wind was blowing.
Ned, the hedgehog, was looking for a home.

He looked down a little hole.
The rabbits said, "This is *our*
home! Look next door."

He looked down a big hole.
The fox said, "This is *my* home!
Look next door."

He looked up in the tree.

Get started

Find the sentences in the story and write the missing words.

1. Ned, the hedgehog, was looking for a _____.

2. He looked _____ a little hole.

3. "This is *our* home! Look _____ door."

4. He _____ down a big hole.

Try these

Answer these questions. Use the story to help you.

1. What was the wind doing?

2. What type of animal is Ned?

3. Why was Ned looking down holes?

4. What animals did he meet?

Now try these

1. What do you think Ned saw up in the tree?

2. Draw a picture of Ned looking for a new home.

3. With a partner, choose another animal you know. Draw and label a picture of where it lives.

Simple instructions: 'Hand Play'

From 'Hand Play' by Elspeth Graham

Hand shadow puppets are fun and easy to do.
Get a desk lamp.
Point the lamp at a plain background.
Switch it on.

Lift one hand up to the light. You will see a shadow on the background. Next try to make some shadow shapes.

Make a flying bat.
Cross hands like this.

press

Then link hands and press together.

Keep hands flat out to make the wings.
Make the fingers go up and down to make the wings flap.

Get started

Find the sentences in the instructions and write the missing words.

1. Hand shadow puppets are fun and _____ to do.

2. Get a _____ lamp.

3. Point the lamp at a _____ background.

4. Lift one hand up to the _____.

Try these

Answer these questions. Use the instructions to help you.

1. What are fun and easy to do?

2. Where should you point the lamp?

3. What will you see on the background?

4. What animal do the instructions tell you to make?

Now try these

1. Do you think making hand shadow puppets would be fun? Why or why not?

2. Draw and label a picture of two friends making hand shadow puppets.

3. With a partner, make hand shadow puppets. Draw a picture to show the shadow shapes you made.

Traditional tales: 'The Fox and the Stork'

From 'The Fox and the Stork' by Simon Puttock

Get started

Find the sentences in the story and write the missing words.

1. Come and dine with _____, Stork.

2. I'll play a _____ on Stork.

3. Come and _____ with me, Fox.

4. I'll show Fox! I'll _____ a trick too!

Try these

Answer these questions. Use the story to help you.

1. Who asked Stork to come for dinner?

2. Who asked Fox to come for dinner?

3. How did Fox play a trick on Stork?

4. How did Stork play a trick on Fox?

Now try these

1. Do you think Fox and Stork are friends? Why or why not?

2. Draw a picture of Fox cooking soup. What has he put in the soup? Write a list.

3. With a partner, make a card saying 'Sorry' from Fox to Stork. Draw a picture on the front.

Traditional tales: 'The Lion and the Mouse'

From 'The Lion and the Mouse' by Anthony Robinson

A lion was sleeping.
A mouse was playing.

The lion opened his eyes.
He saw the mouse.

The lion let the mouse go.

The mouse saw the lion.
He was in a net.

The mouse bit the net.
The lion was free!

Get started

Find the sentences in the story and write the missing words.

1. A lion was _____.

2. A mouse was _____.

3. The lion let the mouse _____.

4. The mouse _____ the net.

Try these

Answer these questions. Use the story to help you.

1. Who caught the mouse?

2. How was the lion trapped?

3. How did the mouse help the lion?

4. What did the lion say to the mouse when he was free?

Now try these

1. Why do you think the mouse helped the lion?

2. Draw a picture of the mouse helping to free the lion.

3. Draw a picture of you helping someone. Explain the picture to a partner. Then write a sentence about what you were doing.

Rhymes and poems: 'Time for School'

From 'Time for School' by Wendy Cope

Time for school, so here I come.
Hello teacher. Bye-bye Mum.

Hello friends. Another day –
Hours and hours to work and play.

Books to read and sums to do,
Stories, painting pictures too.

When the bell rings, we go out,
Run around and laugh and shout.

Then back in through the classroom door.
We're quiet again. We work some more.

Get started

Find the lines in the poem and write the missing words.

    1. Time for _____, so here I come.

    2. Hello teacher. Bye-bye _____.

    3. Books to read and _____ to do.

    4. Stories, painting _____ too.

Try these

Answer these questions. Use the poem to help you.

1. Where is the speaker going at the start of the poem?

2. Who does the speaker say hello to?

3. What does the speaker do when the bell rings?

4. How does the speaker behave in the classroom?

Now try these

1. Do you think the speaker likes school? Why do you think that?

2. Draw a picture of the speaker at school.

3. As a class, say the poem aloud. Repeat the poem and try to remember the words when your teacher pauses.

   Then write down the pairs of words that sound the same. Read the pairs of words aloud to a partner. With your partner, add other words that sound like them.

Story: 'Zog and Zebra'

From 'Zog and Zebra' by Mal Peet and Elspeth Graham

"I am Zog," said Zog.
"My name is Zebra," said Zebra.
"I like your stripes," said Zog. "Have some of my picnic."

After lunch Zog and Zebra went to play.
"Shall we play hide and seek?" asked Zebra.
"You hide and I will count to ten," said Zog.

Zebra hid in the trees. Zog looked for Zebra. His stripes made him hard to see.

Next Zog hid. He was very quiet and very still.

Get started

Find the sentences in the story and write the missing words.

1. "I like your _____," said Zog.

2. After lunch Zog and Zebra went to _____.

3. "You hide and I will _____ to ten," said Zog.

4. Zebra _____ in the trees.

Try these

Answer these questions. Use the story to help you.

1. Who played hide and seek?
2. Who hid first?
3. To what number did Zog count?
4. Why was Zebra hard to see?

Now try these

1. Where do you think Zog would hide?
2. Draw a picture of Zog hiding.
3. Draw a picture of Zebra counting to ten. Work with a partner to add the numbers he counts.

Key stories: 'The Lonely Penguin'

From 'The Lonely Penguin' by Petr Horáček

Crunch crunch! Who's coming through the snow?
It's Penguin. He's lonely.

Crunch crunch! Penguin's looking for his friends.
He can't think where they can be.

Crunch crunch! Penguin's running through the snow.
He's sliding on the frosty ice.

Crunch crunch!
Penguin's looking everywhere.
Penguin climbs up the hill.
Are his friends at the top?

Get started

Find the lines in the story and write the missing words.

    1. Who's coming through the _____?

    2. It's Penguin. He's _____.

    3. Penguin _____ up the hill.

    4. Are his _____ at the top?

Try these

Answer these questions. Use the story to help you.

1. What noise did Penguin make in the snow?

2. Who was Penguin looking for?

3. What was Penguin sliding on?

4. What does Penguin climb?

Now try these

1. Why do you think Penguin was looking for his friends?

2. Draw a picture of Penguin looking for his friends.

3. With a partner, list places that Penguin could look for his friends. Draw and label a map showing all the places Penguin has looked and could look for his friends.

Key stories: 'Bart the Shark'

From 'Bart the Shark' by Paul Shipton

A little pink crab came up to the little green fish.
"Who is Bart the Shark?" she said.

The little green fish said,
"Bart the Shark has a big black fin
and lots of teeth in a horrid grin!"
Then she swam off and hid in a cave.

But the little pink crab did not hide.
"I am not afraid of Bart the Shark," she said.
Then a big, dark shape swam up.
It was Bart the Shark!

Get started

Find the sentences in the story and write the missing words.

1. Bart the Shark has a big _____ fin

2. and lots of _____ in a horrid grin!

3. Then she swam off and hid in a _____.

4. But the little pink _____ did not hide.

Try these

Answer these questions. Use the story to help you.

1. What colour is the little fish?

2. What did the little fish do?

3. Why didn't the little pink crab hide?

4. What was the big, dark shape?

Now try these

1. Why do you think the little pink crab wasn't afraid of Bart the Shark?

2. Draw and label a picture of Bart the Shark, using what the fish said.

3. Draw a picture of the little green fish and the little pink crab talking again. With a partner, decide what they are saying this time. Add speech bubbles to your picture to show what they say.

Fairy stories: 'Jack and the Beanstalk'

From 'Jack and the Beanstalk' by Caryl Hart

Jack and Mum were poor.
Jack sold Daisy for some beans.

Mum was cross.

A beanstalk grew!
Jack climbed up and up.

At the top, Jack found gold!
But a giant found Jack.

The giant was happy.
He grew a beanstalk too!

Mum was happy.

Get started

Find the sentences in the story and write the missing words.

1. Jack and Mum were _____.

2. Jack sold Daisy for some _____.

3. Jack climbed _____ and up.

4. At the top, Jack found _____!

Try these

Answer these questions. Use the story to help you.

1. Who did Jack sell?

2. How did Mum feel when Jack got beans?

3. Who found Jack at the top of the beanstalk?

4. What did the giant grow?

Now try these

1. Why was it good that Jack and the giant swapped?

2. Draw a picture of Jack selling Daisy for some beans.

3. Draw and label a picture of the giant and Jack at the end of the story. With a partner, plan what could happen next in the story. Add a sentence to your picture to explain the plan.

Fairy stories: 'The Prince and the Parsnip'

From 'The Prince and the Parsnip' by Vivian French

Princess Sue wanted to marry a prince.

But Sue wanted to find a prince with feelings. She wanted a kind and caring prince.
Sue wrote letters to ten princes.
"Please come and stay in the palace!"

Princess Sue pulled up ten parsnips from the garden.
When the beds were ready, she set a test. She hid a parsnip under each pillow.

Get started

Find the sentences in the story and write the missing words.

1. Princess Sue wanted to _____ a prince.
2. "Please come and stay in the _____!"
3. Princess Sue pulled up ten _____ from the garden.
4. When the beds were ready, she set a _____.

Try these

Answer these questions. Use the story to help you.

1. What type of prince did Princess Sue want to marry?
2. How many princes did she invite to the palace?
3. Where did she get the parsnips?
4. Where did she hide the parsnips?

Now try these

1. Why do you think Princess Sue was hiding parsnips under the pillows?
2. Draw a picture of Princess Sue pulling up parsnips in the garden.
3. Draw a picture of some of the princes going to bed with the parsnips under their pillows. With a partner, talk about what could happen next. Add a sentence to your picture to explain what you think.

Traditional tales: 'The Hare and the Tortoise'

From 'The Hare and the Tortoise' by Melanie Williamson

Hare said to Tortoise, "I'm so much bigger and better than you." Tortoise said, "Bigger doesn't always mean better."

They both said, "Let's have a race." Hare thought he was so much better than Tortoise that he gave him a head start.

Slow coach!

Hare ran past Tortoise.

Hare had time to eat. Hare had time to play.

Hare had time to snooze...

Get started

Find the sentences in the tale and write the missing words.

1. Tortoise said, "_____ doesn't always mean better."

2. Hare thought he was so much _____ than Tortoise that he gave him a head start.

3. Hare ran past _____.

4. Hare had _____ to eat.

Try these

Answer these questions. Use the tale and picture to help you.

1. Which animal was bigger?

2. What did Tortoise say back to Hare?

3. What did they decide to do?

4. What did Hare call Tortoise during the race?

Now try these

1. Who do you think wins the race? Why?

2. Draw a picture of Hare playing.

3. Draw a picture of Hare running past Tortoise. With a partner, talk about what Tortoise is thinking. Add a sentence to your picture to show what Tortoise thinks.

Reading reports: 'The Rainforest at Night'

From 'The Rainforest at Night' by Nic Bishop

When it gets dark in the rainforest, things start to happen.

Bats wake up and fly in the night. The bats sleep in the day under a leaf.

At night they zip and zoom in the sky to chase moths and insects.

A bat can flip a moth into its mouth with its wings.

A hungry bat will eat a hundred insects in a night.

Get started

Find the sentences in the report and write the missing words.

1. When it gets dark in the _____, things start to happen.

2. Bats wake up and _____ in the night.

3. The bats _____ in the day under a leaf.

4. A bat can flip a moth into its _____ with its wings.

Try these

Answer these questions. Use the report to help you.

1. When do bats wake up and fly?

2. Where do bats sleep in the day?

3. What do bats chase at night?

4. How many insects will a hungry bat eat in a night?

Now try these

1. Why do you think bats might fly in the night and sleep in the day?

2. Draw a bat sleeping under a leaf in the day.

3. Draw and label a picture of a bat chasing insects. With a partner, list insects the bat could eat. Add the list to your picture.

Reading reports: 'The Sun and the Moon'

From 'The Sun and the Moon' by Paul Shipton

The Sun is very big. It is made of very, very hot gas. The Sun is a star.

The Moon is not as big as our planet.
The land is very rocky.
There are no animals or plants.

All of our light and heat comes from the Sun.
The Sun is much too hot to visit.

Some men did visit the Moon in a rocket.

Our planet travels around the Sun.

Get started

Find the sentences in the report and write the missing words.

1. The Sun is very _____.

2. The Sun is a _____.

3. The Moon is not as big as our _____.

4. The _____ is very rocky.

Try these

Answer these questions. Use the report to help you.

1. What is the Sun made of?

2. What is the land like on the Moon?

3. Are there animals or plants on the Moon?

4. Why can't people visit the Sun?

Now try these

1. Why do you think people wanted to visit the Moon?

2. Draw and label a picture of the Sun, the Moon and our planet, Earth.

3. Draw a picture of some men visiting the Moon. With a partner, come up with two sentences to show what the men could be saying.